I'M GOOD AT ENGLISH

WHAT JOB CAN I GET?

Richard Spilsbury

First published in paperback in 2012
by Wayland

Wayland
Hachette Children's Books
338 Euston Road
London NW1 3BH

Wayland Australia
Level 17/207 Kent Street,
Sydney, NSW 2000

Commissioning editor: Camilla Lloyd
Project editor: Kelly Davis
Designer: Tim Mayer, MayerMedia
Picture research: Richard Spilsbury/
Alice Harman
Proofreader and indexer: Alice Harman

Produced for Wayland by
White-Thomson Publishing Ltd
www.wtpub.co.uk
+44 (0)843 2087 460

British Library Cataloguing in Publication Data

Spilsbury, Richard, 1963-
I'm good at – what job can I get?.
English.
1. English language–Vocational guidance–Juvenile literature.
I. Title
428'.0023-dc22

ISBN: 978 0 7502 7096 0

First published in 2011 by Wayland

Wayland is a division of Hachette Children's
Books, an Hachette UK company
www.hachette.co.uk

Printed in China

Picture credits
1, Shutterstock/maureenplainfield; 3, Dreamstime/Icefields; 4, Dreamstime/Janahorova; 5, Dreamstime/Inbj; 6, Dreamstime/Seragal; 7, Shutterstock/CandyBoxPhoto; 8, Dreamstime/Goruppa; 9, Dreamstime/Sophieso; 10, Shutterstock/maureenplainfield; 11, Shutterstock/Brenda Carson; 12, Dreamstime/Trombax; 13, iStock/TonyBaggett; 14, Shutterstock/Gemenacom; 15, Dreamstime/Moiseev; 16, Dreamstime/Endostock; 17, Dreamstime/Zairbek Mansurov; 18, Dreamstime/Stylephotographs; 19, Dreamstime/Poco_bw; 20, Dreamstime/Bcnewell; 21, Dreamstime/Junial; 22 Dreamstime/Lincolnrogers; 23, Dreamstime/Samrat35; 24, Dreamstime/Icefields; 25, Dreamstime/Photovibes; 26, Dreamstime/Engraver; 27, Dreamstime/Monkeybusinessimages; 28, Dreamstime/Smilla; 29, Dreamstime/Sebcz; cover (top left), Dreamstime/Goruppa; cover (top right), Dreamstime/Monkeybusinessimages; cover (bottom), Dreamstime/Endostock.

CONTENTS

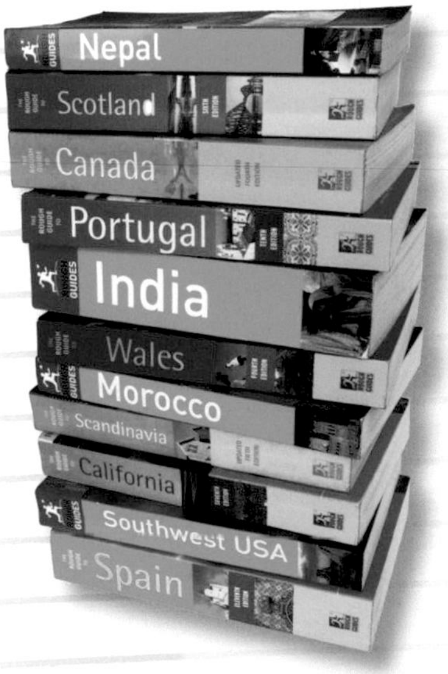

The world of English

If you are good at English, you will have a vast range of career options. Writing accurately and effectively and using a wide vocabulary will make it easy for you to communicate and pass on information. As an English student, you study literature and language, and develop analytical and creative skills. Most English courses involve presentations and discussions that also develop good speaking skills. Being able to analyse, write and communicate is valuable for almost every job.

By reading a wide range of books, you improve your knowledge and become good at assessing what different texts mean.

English in the workplace

Workers in many professions need English skills, not just the more obvious ones like authors and journalists. Business managers need to know how to handle large amounts of information in critical and creative ways. Shopkeepers need to be able to communicate clearly with customers. People in marketing or advertising jobs need to know how to write persuasively. And even scientists conducting experiments need to be able to write clear reports explaining their results.

Special skills

English skills are in demand. Indeed, English exam passes are a basic requirement for continuing on to A-Levels, degrees and many different careers. If you are good at English, you already have a range of skills that will be very useful in future jobs. When writing essays about books, you learn to come up with arguments and explain your ideas in a clear, logical and structured way. If you study English later, at college or university, you will develop these skills even further. These special skills are transferable to many jobs and industries – this book introduces just a few of them.

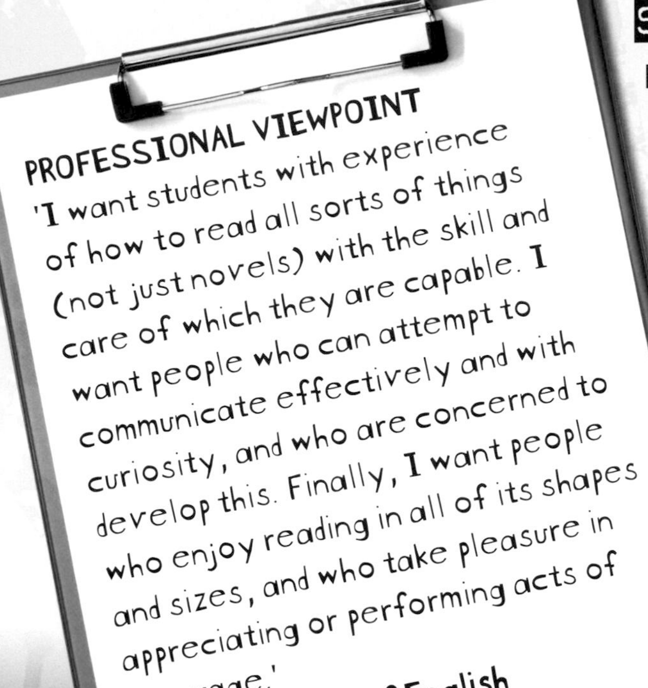

PROFESSIONAL VIEWPOINT

'I want students with experience of how to read all sorts of things (not just novels) with the skill and care of which they are capable. I want people who can attempt to communicate effectively and with curiosity, and who are concerned to develop this. Finally, I want people who enjoy reading in all of its shapes and sizes, and who take pleasure in appreciating or performing acts of language.'

Rick, professor of English

Around 1.5 billion people speak English, making it one of the most widely spoken and read languages in the world.

Advertising copywriter

Copywriters create the words used in adverts and other kinds of publicity. They write slogans and phrases like 'Just Do It' (Nike) or 'A Diamond is Forever' (De Beers) to draw the public's attention to a particular product, business, group or idea. Copywriters usually work in teams at advertising agencies or within advertising departments of big businesses.

PROFESSIONAL VIEWPOINT

'Agencies look for individuals to have an interest in what makes people "tick" and for them to be self-confident, but at the same time possess the ability to be self-questioning. Equally important is having a passion for advertising and being able to convey that passion.'

Liz, ad agency recruiter

Clear, eye-catching adverts can massively increase sales of a product.

Job description

Advertising copywriters:

- work to briefs and schedules agreed with clients
- research target markets
- come up with ideas with the art director (who provides the visuals)
- present options to clients and tweak ideas until the client is happy
- oversee the production of advertisements.

What skills do I need?

Copywriters need to be creative, have good communication skills and enjoy working in teams. Many copywriters have a Higher National Diploma (HND) or university degree in advertising, design, English or other subjects that show they have writing skills, imagination and creativity. Training for junior copywriters tends to be on the job, but you can also do postgraduate diplomas in copywriting. Copywriting is a competitive career, so it is a good idea to build up a portfolio of ideas or previous projects, to show companies what you can do and what work experience you have.

Different types of copywriter

Copywriters work on adverts for different types of media, such as TV, newspapers, posters, radio and direct mail, and on the Internet or websites. Some copywriters work on viral advertising campaigns. These are Internet promotions using social networking, and they may take the form of video clips, interactive games or text messages. A junior copywriter may progress to senior copywriter to work on more important accounts. Creative directors control a team of copywriters.

Many successful copywriters set up as self-employed freelancers.

Copywriters come up with many different ideas and most are rejected. They have to work with the rest of the team and clients to find the right idea.

Broadcasting researcher

Many TV and radio presenters only sound as if they know what they're talking about because of the work done by broadcasting researchers! Researchers provide the ideas and material for radio, television and online programmes and help with the recording of broadcasts. They might work on news and current affairs, consumer shows, quizzes and talk shows, reality TV shows, dramas or films.

– Job description –

Broadcasting researchers:

- find out facts and figures from various sources
- contact people for comments and interviews
- check radio and TV archives for previous interviews
- find locations to make programmes
- write scripts for presenters to read out.

→ Broadcasters rely on broadcasting researchers to come up with much of the material they use on their shows.

What skills do I need?

TV is a competitive industry, so you need to be very determined to make it as a researcher. You need to be self-motivated, outgoing and have good general knowledge. It is not a requirement for researcher jobs, but most researchers have a degree or HND. Many researchers start out as journalists (see page 12), others as office assistants or runners in broadcast companies. The BBC and some independent companies run training schemes for new entrants.

PROFESSIONAL VIEWPOINT

'You should make it your business to keep up-to-date with news, current affairs and the world around you – how else will you come up with new ideas? TV is an ideas industry after all ... And try and be nice to (or at least grin and bear) everyone you meet in the industry, especially when you're starting out. After all, you never know who could be sitting on your interview panel one day!'

Naphtalia Loderick, researcher on BBC1's *The One Show*

Broadcasting researchers generally work for producers, the people who initiate, co-ordinate and supervise a programme or series. They work with other people too, for example when talking to experts or to members of the public. But researchers also sometimes work alone, for instance when searching archives for information.

Researchers often get the chance to travel, sometimes worldwide, when working at different broadcast locations.

Theatre director

Do you like reading plays and going to the theatre? Do you think you could direct a play? Theatre directors control all the different aspects of putting on a play or show at the theatre. They plan how to stage the written script, and then work to bring the show to life, taking into account the available budget and theatre space.

Job description

Theatre directors:

- work out how to present the script on stage, sometimes alongside writers and playwrights
- attend auditions, interviews and recalls
- cast actors, or work with a casting department
- work with set designers to plan how the stage should look
- work with theatre managers and costume designers to choose set, lighting and costumes
- watch rehearsals, instructing actors on how to improve their performance.

Directors are responsible for all aspects of a theatrical show, from the way the lines are spoken to the set design.

Directors work very closely with performers, set and costume designers, choreographers, and lighting engineers. Many theatre directors are freelancers, who work for different theatres on different productions. Others are employed as directors of a particular theatre or drama company, and direct their productions.

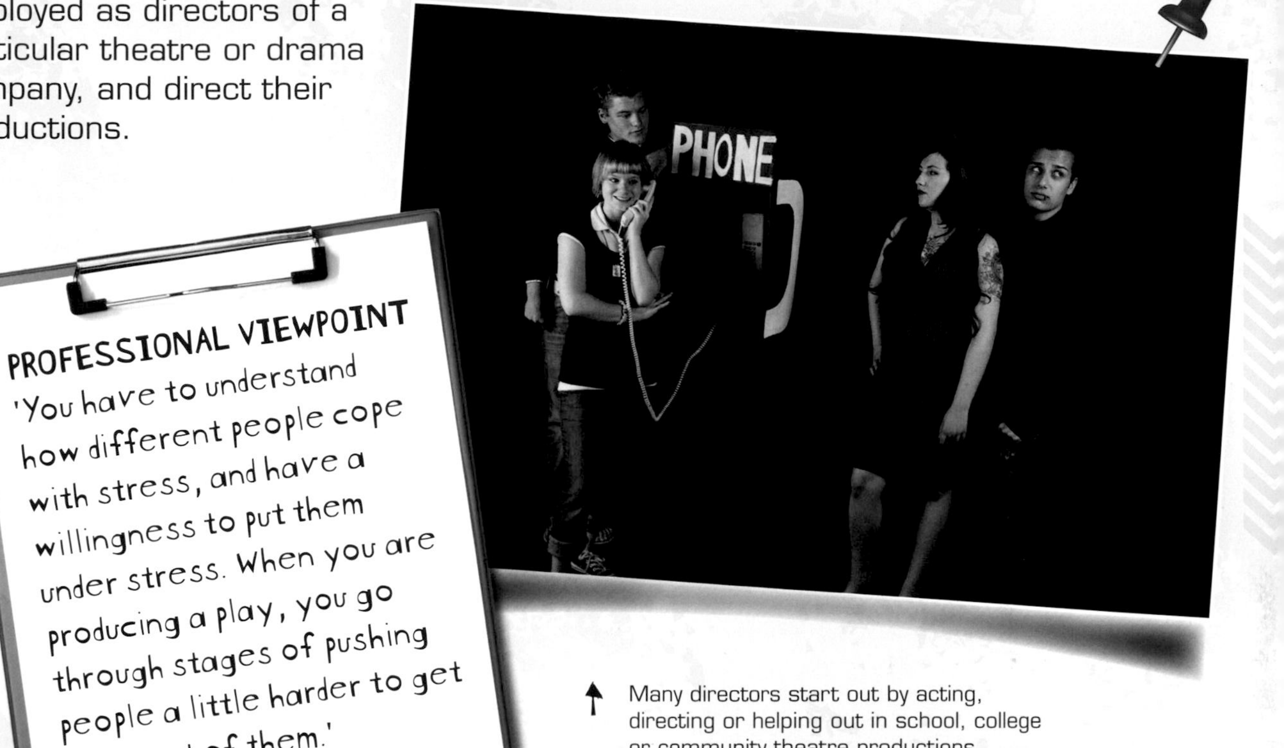

Many directors start out by acting, directing or helping out in school, college or community theatre productions.

PROFESSIONAL VIEWPOINT

'You have to understand how different people cope with stress, and have a willingness to put them under stress. When you are producing a play, you go through stages of pushing people a little harder to get more out of them.'

Richard, director

What skills do I need?

Theatre directors should be creative, able to visualise how to put on a written show, and good with people. It helps to be interested in theatre history, and to have read and seen a wide variety of plays and shows. Some directors make it through practical experience alone. For example, they may move into directing from acting. Many directors have a university degree or HND in English, drama, theatre studies, music or creative/performing arts. However, work in theatre is highly competitive so it is important to get as much experience as you can in acting, stage management and direction.

Newspaper journalist

Journalists have to be quick at thinking of questions that will get the most interesting information from interviewees.

Journalists are responsible for reporting news on topics ranging from world affairs to sports results. Newspaper journalists gather, interpret and present news (and other items of current interest) in written reports for local and national newspapers. They usually start out working on a variety of news subjects for one paper, and when experienced may specialise in writing features on a particular subject area.

Job description

Newspaper journalists:

- find and research the background to stories
- conduct interviews, and attend events and meetings to gather news
- write accurate reports to tight deadlines in a fixed number of words
- help to choose pictures to accompany articles
- tweak written pieces until they are approved by the editors who put newspapers together.

PROFESSIONAL VIEWPOINT

'You may think you need to be a great writer or a fast typist to become a journalist. But you just need to be outgoing and brave enough to talk to people you don't know, and imaginative. You have to be ready for a change and ready to take on a challenge.'

Meimei, journalist

What skills do I need?

Journalists need to be interested in current affairs and be good at assessing the important points in a story. They should also be able to write them up quickly, clearly and be able to engage their audience. They need to be persuasive so that people will tell them things, and also tenacious – getting a job on a newspaper is very competitive. Experience helps, so many journalists start by volunteering on local newspapers. Most take a university degree in journalism or English, followed by a training course in journalism, such as those accredited by the National Council for the Training of Journalists (NCTJ).

Different types of journalist

Magazine journalists write for local, national and international magazines. Some cover many topics but others are for people with particular interests such as photography or surfing. Some journalists write text for online versions of papers or magazines. Other journalists work in TV and radio broadcasting, either gathering news for others to read out, or reporting the news themselves.

Journalists must work to tight deadlines to get daily newspapers out on time for people to buy them.

Archivist

Are you the sort of person who does not like to throw things out because they might be important records of the past? If so, maybe you could be an archivist.

Archivists are good at reading, analysing and sorting information.

Job description

Archivists:

- liaise with people who are providing original material for an archive
- decide which documents to archive and which to reject
- make sure archive material is organised logically
- catalogue and index material so that people can locate specific items
- store and handle original fragile material carefully, both in the archive and when lent out
- arrange talks, visits and exhibitions.

Archives are stores of documents, letters, books, photos, films and other materials, either as hard copies or digital formats saved on computers, or both. Archivists are the people who collect, sort and look after archives that have historical importance for individuals, organisations and nations. Archivists preserve these important records, and help researchers and journalists find the information they need.

What skills do I need?

Archivists have an interest in history and preserving records. They are also skilled at researching, analysing and sorting information, and good at IT. There are a lot of archives, so there are many job opportunities for an archivist. Most archivists have a university degree, often in English or history, followed by a qualification or second degree in archives and records management. Many archivists start off as volunteers or as trainee archivists in a local archive.

PROFESSIONAL VIEWPOINT

'What I enjoy about archiving is that you never know what you'll come across in the material – there's always something new and unexpected.'

Anna, archivist

Different types of archivist

Archivists may work with a variety of different archives. These could be for local and national governments, businesses, charities, universities, hospitals, museums or individuals, such as archives of famous people's writings and possessions. The National Archives hold census records from the past that include ancient manuscripts, World War I diaries and six million historical maps; and the Hulton Archive has an extensive collection of photographs from the 1930s onwards.

Archivists preserve material such as old photos that provide original evidence about people and stories from the past. →

Public relations officer

Public relations (PR) officers enhance an individual's or company's reputation and image. They find ways of getting positive information about their client into the media to win support for them or their business. For example, PR officers for the charity Cancer Research create campaigns to raise funds for medical research and awareness of the disease, for example by writing leaflets about patients' experiences.

– Job description –

Public relations officers:

- plan public relations campaigns
- write press releases, articles, blogs, news releases and speeches
- organise and give press briefings, conferences, exhibitions, receptions and tours
- answer enquiries from individuals, journalists and organisations
- need to be informed so they know if their client's reputation is in trouble
- create and maintain useful contacts in the media.

Most public relations officers work with a team of marketing staff to brainstorm ideas for a campaign.

Different types of public relations officer

Some public relations officers work with high-profile people such as celebrities or politicians, arranging interviews, sending out press releases (or statements) and even giving interviews to journalists. Some work for businesses, for example arranging launch events for a new product or persuading journalists to review the product in their magazine. Online PR officers use blogs or social networking to promote their company to a target audience.

PROFESSIONAL VIEWPOINT

'Getting into the arts is very competitive, so I would suggest searching high and low for whatever work experience you can get. I completed an unpaid three-month media and marketing internship for another arts organisation before I got my current job.'

Elsie, public relations officer

Former world number one tennis star Jim Courier hosts a PR event promoting the Tennis Legends tour for older players.

What skills do I need?

Public relations officers need to be able to write and speak confidently and clearly. Many gain useful experience by getting involved in school and college magazines and debating societies. PR people need to be persistent and persuasive. Many PR officers have a university degree in a subject such as English, media studies or advertising, and sometimes a postgraduate diploma or qualification in public relations or marketing. Large companies may take on and train graduates within their PR departments.

Librarian

Librarians store, catalogue and arrange loans of books, magazines, CDs and DVDs, and provide sources of information on computers. Librarians may work in public libraries in town and city centres, or in more limited-access university, college and school libraries. They may even work in private libraries belonging to large companies or individual collectors.

Job description

Librarians:
- choose and order new books and resources for the library
- advise library users about resources and materials and how to access them
- classify and index resource materials on digital catalogues
- organise events such as school visits, writing workshops and author readings
- manage the library and its budget.

Librarians use English and IT skills to help people explore and locate their resources.

What skills do I need?

Librarians usually love different kinds of books and keep up-to-date with new publications. They need good IT skills as well as literacy and numeracy, and should enjoy interacting with others. Library assistants need GCSE passes to start work, but most librarians have a university degree and a postgraduate qualification accredited by the Chartered Institute of Library and Information Professionals (CILIP). As for any career, it helps if you can get work experience, so asking if you can help out at your school library would be a good start.

PROFESSIONAL VIEWPOINT

'The job is changing all the time and you get satisfaction from helping people find information on the Internet as well as in books. Above all, I love being able to recommend books and other sources that I know people will find exciting.'

Nikki, librarian

Different types of librarian

In public libraries, librarians order, organise and make available different resources for the community. Librarians in large libraries may be in charge of training and managing staff. Library assistants work for librarians; for example, they organise book repairs and give out fines for overdue books. In small, specialist libraries, librarians work alone and have good background knowledge of the specialist subject of the library.

Think how hard it would be to find a specific source of information in this library if there were no librarian to organise it! →

Legal clerk

Legal clerks work in law offices of private law firms or in government law courts. Their job is to help lawyers or judges on different law cases. They research the laws and the facts surrounding a case, and brief a judge or lawyer on any action that should be taken. Clerks make important decisions, based on evidence, which can affect people's finances or freedom.

Job description

Legal clerks:

- research legal documents to investigate the facts, so they can inform a judge or lawyer about possible ways to proceed in a court case
- prepare and file documents, and write letters to parties involved in the case
- read and report on any new documents that come up in the case
- make sure important documents are delivered to people involved in the case
- try to sort out disputes between different parties (sides) in a case.

If you are intrigued by trials and like helping people, becoming a legal clerk could be the job for you.

Legal clerks help lawyers and judges make important decisions.

Different types of legal clerk

Legal clerks work on different types of cases depending on the law firm they work for. If they work in a family law firm, they will often work on divorce cases, for example advising clients about the grounds (reasons) they should use to file for divorce. Legal clerks in a criminal law firm work on cases involving a crime, such as burglary. Commercial law firms work for companies and businesses, for example sorting out insurance disputes.

PROFESSIONAL VIEWPOINT

'Academic ability is necessary to progress to the higher levels of the profession. You must develop a decisive and determined nature, as the decisions you make may not be popular with some members of chambers. Going through the motions is not sufficient. The old cliché of "going the extra mile" does work!'

Colin, legal clerk

What skills do I need?

You need to know the English language very well to be able to read, understand and write complex legal documents. Many legal clerks are law students at university or new graduates. By working on different cases, they get useful experience for a future job as a lawyer. Some clerks start as legal secretaries, typing up letters and reports, and learn legal clerical skills as they progress.

Author

Do you like writing stories, descriptions or instructions? If so, perhaps you would like to be an author. Authors are the people who write fiction, such as novels, plays and TV scripts, and non-fiction texts, including textbooks and manuals.

Different types of author

There are many different types of author. Technical authors write the text for manuals and leaflets that help people use different kinds of technology, such as instructions for operating a DVD recorder. Scriptwriters and playwrights write dialogue for actors who appear in radio and TV shows and films. Travel authors write books, and articles for magazines about different places, and give tips for tourists. Most authors write under their own names, but ghostwriters write books that are published under another person's name, for example a celebrity's autobiography.

Some authors help to advertise and to sell their creations by taking part in book signings.

Job description

Authors:

- come up with an idea for a book and may persuade a publisher to publish it
- research information from different sources, including books, websites and interviews
- select and organise material into chapters and themes
- write persuasively, entertainingly and concisely, often to a deadline
- check their work and revise it, depending on an editor's comments (see pages 24–25).

PROFESSIONAL VIEWPOINT
'One of the things I love about my job is that I learn something new every week because I am always researching new topics. One week I might be reading about lions; the next I could be researching climate change.'
Louise, non-fiction author

Authors need to be self-motivated, because most are freelancers and work alone.

What skills do I need?

To be an author, you need to be good at English, and able to research and write clearly. For example, if a novelist sets a book in the 1930s they need to research that period. Authors also need to be creative and able to judge what to put in and leave out. You do not have to have qualifications to be an author, although many writers have a university degree in English language or literature, or a qualification in creative writing. Specialist authors usually have qualifications in their specialist subject, for example a degree in IT if they write software instructions.

Editor

Editors read through an author's text and make sure the content, style and grammar are correct. They discuss corrections, comments and improvements with the author. They follow the progress of the book, from the delivery of the author's work to the publishing house, right through to publication.

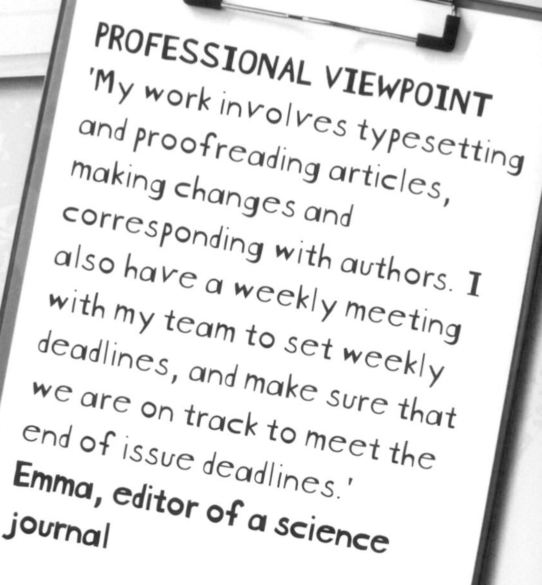

PROFESSIONAL VIEWPOINT
'My work involves typesetting and proofreading articles, making changes and corresponding with authors. I also have a weekly meeting with my team to set weekly deadlines, and make sure that we are on track to meet the end of issue deadlines.'
Emma, editor of a science journal

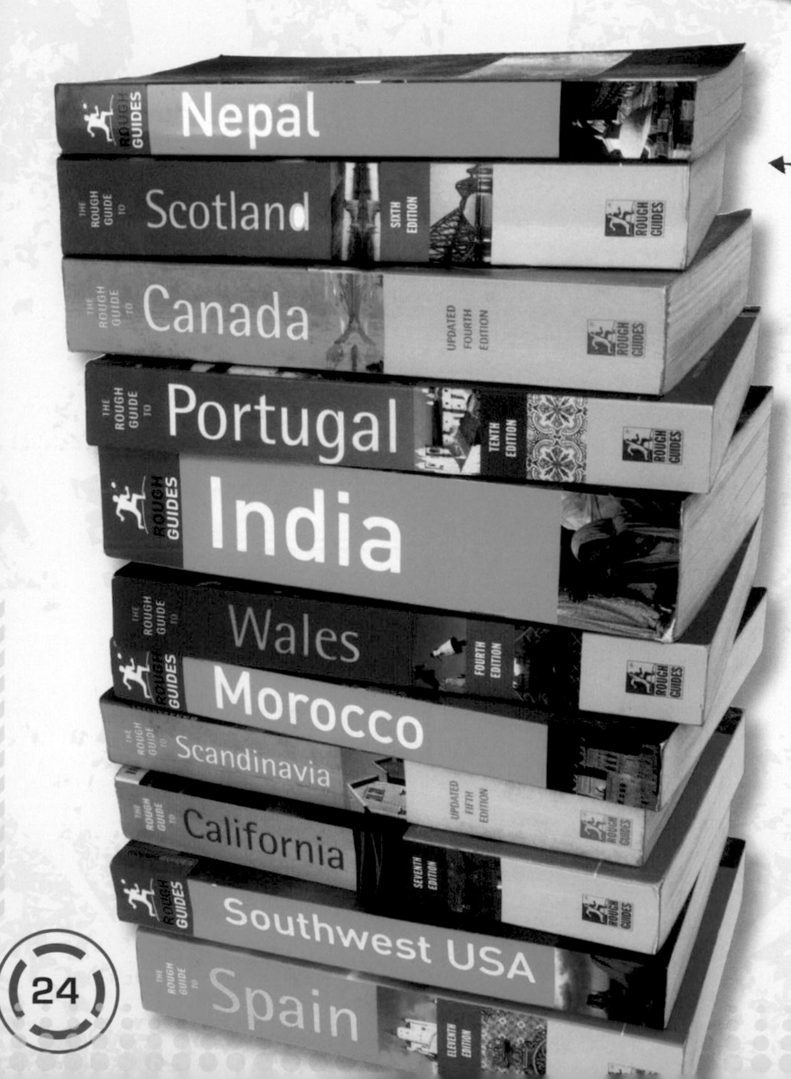

Editors are responsible for the style and content of a wide variety of books.

Different types of editor

Commissioning editors think of ideas for books and find authors to write them, or read authors' ideas for new books and decide which to publish. Copy editors or sub-editors check the sense, spelling, facts and writing style of the text. Proofreaders are editors who do a final read-through of a book before it is published. Web editors format text for websites, using coding languages such as html.

What skills do I need?

Editors need to be good at spelling and grammar, and paying attention to detail. They also need ICT skills and a love of writing. Most editors have a university degree, often in English or journalism. They often start off in a junior role, such as editorial assistant. Editors of specialist books, such as science or economics, may need a degree in that subject. You can also study for qualifications in editorial publishing courses at some institutions.

Job description

Editors:

- check written text for content, grammar, sense, accuracy, style and length
- work with authors to make corrections and improvements to the text
- brief designers on how the book should look
- work with picture editors to choose illustrations for a book
- liaise with other departments, such as marketing and production
- ensure that publications are printed on time
- commission online resources and new editions of previously published books.

Web editors may work on the content and coding of websites that sell products or services, or provide news and information.

Bookseller

Booksellers sell books to people, and help them find a particular book by giving advice based on their knowledge. Some booksellers may work for small independent second-hand bookshops or shops specialising in just art or cookery books, and others for larger high-street chains or online bookstores.

It can be very satisfying to help someone find a book they really enjoy reading.

Different types of bookseller

There are many different types of bookseller. In a second-hand bookstore, booksellers work out the right price for the book they are buying or selling, based on how rare it is and its condition. In large chains, different booksellers may have specialist knowledge of particular types of books and be in charge of separate departments, such as fiction or children's books. They may also be responsible for organising events such as readings by authors. Online booksellers may write book reviews on their websites to encourage people to buy their books, and also post books to customers.

PROFESSIONAL VIEWPOINT

'The best way to learn about bookselling is to work in a bookshop. Even a week or two can give you a sense of the day-to-day realities of the trade, such as dealing with all those unfamiliar faces and demands, working on a till, ordering stock, looking after the existing stock, handling invoices – experiences that are impossible to achieve in any other way.'

Booksellers Association

Job description

Booksellers:

- choose books to sell, with the help of publishers' catalogues and book reviews
- help customers choose the right book
- make orders and take payments for books
- monitor stock levels
- work on budgets, pay for orders, and arrange deliveries and returns
- sort books on shelves and create interesting displays.

In a bookshop, adults and children have a chance to see a wide range of titles, and to look inside the books before they buy them.

What skills do I need?

A bookseller should have good selling skills, be confident using computers and databases, and have an interest in books and literature. Booksellers will usually read a lot of books themselves, and enjoy recommending books to others. Most training is carried out on the job, so there are no set academic requirements for working as a bookseller, but most booksellers have GCSEs in English and maths and many also have a university degree.

English teacher

Are you so good at English that you would like to pass on your skills to others? English teachers often teach people how to read and write, and other basic literacy skills. They may also teach more complex skills, such as analysis of language use or literary criticism of novels or poems.

PROFESSIONAL VIEWPOINT

'Patience is what I have had to learn the most, and a sense of humour really does help get you through the day. The ability to inspire and make a connection with the students, by relating the subject to real life and making it relevant to their experiences, is really important.'

Christine, secondary school English teacher

English lecturers carefully prepare and plan materials to present in their lectures at colleges and universities.

Teaching English as a foreign language is rewarding and a great way to experience different cultures and places.

Different types of English teacher

At primary school, teachers tend to teach a range of subjects to one class, and one teacher may take responsibility for the way the whole school teaches the English or literacy curriculum. At secondary school, teachers can teach purely English, either as a class teacher or a head of department. At A-level, English teachers may specialise further, teaching either English literature or English language. At university, lecturers in English may specialise in particular types or periods of literature, and do research on their own books and essays. Some English teachers teach English as a foreign language (TEFL) to people whose first language is not English, and often work abroad.

What skills do I need?

To teach English, you need good communication and leadership skills, and great enthusiasm for English. You should also be adaptable when teaching pupils of different abilities, even those who don't want to learn. Most English teachers have a university degree in education, or a degree in English language or literature and a Postgraduate Certificate of Education (PGCE). If you wish to teach English as a foreign language, you usually need to get a specialist certificate.

Job description

English teachers:

- plan lessons
- teach classes in a way that engages the pupils
- keep order and discipline
- mark coursework, essays and exam papers
- talk to pupils about their work and other issues
- communicate well with parents and with other staff at school, college or university
- keep records and written reports about children's progress.

Glossary

advertising communication through words and design intended to draw attention to a product, service or cause

advertising agency company specialising in creating advertising campaigns for different companies or organisations

analytical using a logical method of thinking about something in order to understand it

audition sample performance, for example by an actor or singer in order to get a role

broadcasting business of making and transmitting TV and radio programmes

budget summary of costs and income for an individual, business or organisation that is used to make financial plans

cast performers in a play or other production

choreographer person who creates sequences of dance moves and instructs dancers how to perform them

current affairs type of broadcasting that analyses and discusses in detail recent or ongoing news stories

digital formats ways of storing words, images and other information on computers, such as .doc, .pdf or .jpg files

feature special, important or lengthy article in a magazine or newspaper

freelancer someone who works independently on paid jobs for different employers

hard copy print-out of material originally created in digital format

lawyer qualified professional adviser on the law, who represents different clients in legal cases

lighting engineer person who designs and sets up lighting for live and recorded shows, concerts, films and other events

literary criticism written evaluation, interpretation or questioning of a work of fiction

marketing business of finding out what people want to buy and how to sell things to them

media means of communication that reaches a large number of people, e.g. radio, TV, newspapers

press briefing interview or meeting giving information to journalists

press release written or recorded statement or information about something or someone with possible interest for the media

runner general assistant in broadcasting or film production with jobs ranging from carrying equipment to taking messages

set scenery or background for a play, show or other performance

social networking sharing information and communication among members of online communities, for example using websites such as Facebook

vocabulary set of words a person understands and uses

Further information

There are many specific courses, apprenticeships and jobs using English skills, so where do you go to find out more? It is really useful to meet up with careers advisers at school or college, and to attend careers fairs to see the range of opportunities. Remember that public libraries and newspapers are other important sources of information. The earlier you check out your options, the better prepared you will be to put your English skills to good use as you earn a living in future.

Books

Career Ideas for Kids Who Like Writing (Career Ideas for Kids), Diane Lindsay Reeves, Facts On File Inc, 2001

Careers and Jobs in the Media, Simon Kent, Kogan Page, 2005

English (Discovering Careers for Your Future), Infobase Publishing, Facts On File Inc, 2006

Radio and Television (Discovering Careers for Your Future), Infobase Publishing, Facts On File Inc, 2008

So You Want to Be a Film or TV Screenwriter? (Careers in Film and Television), Amy Dunkleberger, Enslow, 2007

What Next After School?: All You Need to Know About Work, Travel and Study (Times), Elizabeth Holmes, Kogan Page, 2009

Websites

www.prospects.ac.uk/options_english_job_options.htm
This is a useful guide to your job options. It is aimed at English graduates but it gives a clear idea of what routes to take for careers using English. There is also a comprehensive list of resources and contacts on this site.

www.lawcareers.net/information/firststeps.aspx
Do you want to have a career in law? Find out more at this UK site.

www.skillset.org/publishing/careers/job_profiles
A website with some clearly organised information about publishing roles, from writer to bookseller, media researcher to proofreader.

www.wetfeet.com/Careers-and-Industries/Careers/Marketing.aspx
A helpful summary of marketing careers, requirements, career tracks, and the state of the global job market. Go to the same URL and replace the word 'Marketing' with 'Advertising' or 'Editorial-and-Writing' to discover more about two other types of career.

Index